CFP® Certification Exam Flashcard Review Book

Retirement & Employee Benefits

Written by
Matthew Brandeburg, CFP®

A publication of
Coventry House Publishing

ISBN: 1733591184
ISBN-13: 978-1733591188

CONTENTS

CFP® Certification Exam Flashcard Review Book: Retirement & Employee Benefits

RETIREMENT PLANNING

RETIREMENT NEEDS CALCULATION: FUTURE VALUE OF REQUIRED INCOME

RETIREMENT NEEDS CALCULATION: PRESENT VALUE OF SERIAL PAYMENTS

RETIREMENT NEEDS CALCULATION: FUTURE VALUE OF REQUIRED INCOME

Step 1: Calculate the future value of required income during the first year of retirement
- End mode
- PV = Required annual income in today's dollars
- i = Inflation rate
- n = Number of years until retirement
- PMT = 0
- Solve for FV

RETIREMENT NEEDS CALCULATION: PRESENT VALUE OF SERIAL PAYMENTS

Step 2: Calculate the present value of serial payments
- Begin mode
- PMT = The FV from step 1 becomes the PMT for step 2
- i = Inflation adjusted return: [(1 + return) / (1 + inflation rate)] − 1
- n = Number of years from retirement until death
- FV = 0
- Solve for PV

RETIREMENT NEEDS CALCULATION:
AMOUNT NEEDED IN TODAY'S DOLLARS

AVERAGE INDEXED
MONTHLY EARNINGS (AIME)

RETIREMENT NEEDS CALCULATION: AMOUNT NEEDED IN TODAY'S DOLLARS

Step 3: Calculate the total amount needed to fund retirement in today's dollars
- End mode
- FV =The PV from step 2 becomes the FV for step 3
- i = Investment return
- n = Number of years until retirement
- PMT = 0
- Solve for PV

AVERAGE INDEXED MONTHLY EARNINGS (AIME)

- Social security retirement benefits are calculated using a worker's average indexed monthly earnings (AIME)
- AIME summarizes up to 35 years of a worker's indexed earnings
- AIME is used to calculate a worker's primary insurance amount (PIA)

PRIMARY INSURANCE AMOUNT (PIA)

SOCIAL SECURITY QUARTERS OF COVERAGE

PRIMARY INSURANCE
AMOUNT (PIA)

- Primary insurance amount (PIA) is the social security retirement benefit an individual will receive if he or she elects to begin receiving benefits at full retirement age
- For married couples, each spouse is entitled to receive a social security retirement benefit based on the greater of his or her own benefit, or 50% of the spouse's benefit

---

SOCIAL SECURITY
QUARTERS OF COVERAGE

- A worker is "fully insured" if he or she has earned at least 40 quarters of coverage
- A worker is "currently insured" if he or she has earned at least 6 quarters of coverage during the previous 13 calendar quarters
- A maximum of four quarters of coverage (credits) may be earned in a single calendar year
- Earnings needed to earn one social security credit is $1,360 in 2019

SOCIAL SECURITY
FULL RETIREMENT AGE

SOCIAL SECURITY
FULL RETIREMENT AGE

SOCIAL SECURITY
FULL RETIREMENT AGE

- Full retirement age for an individual born in the year 1937 or earlier is age 65
  - If born in 1938, full retirement age is 65 and 2 months
  - If born in 1939, full retirement age is 65 and 4 months
  - If born in 1940, full retirement age is 65 and 6 months
  - If born in 1941, full retirement age is 65 and 8 months
  - If born in 1942, full retirement age is 65 and 10 months

SOCIAL SECURITY
FULL RETIREMENT AGE

- Full retirement age for an individual born between the years 1943 and 1954 is age 66
  - If born in 1955, full retirement age is 66 and 2 months
  - If born in 1956, full retirement age is 66 and 4 months
  - If born in 1957, full retirement age is 66 and 6 months
  - If born in 1958, full retirement age is 66 and 8 months
  - If born in 1959, full retirement age is 66 and 10 months
- Full retirement age for an individual born in the year 1960 or later is age 67

REDUCED SOCIAL SECURITY BENEFITS FOR EARLY RETIREMENT

INCREASED SOCIAL SECURITY BENEFITS FOR DELAYED RETIREMENT

REDUCED SOCIAL SECURITY BENEFITS FOR EARLY RETIREMENT

- A fully insured worker may elect to receive social security retirement benefits early, but with a permanently reduced monthly benefit
- Benefits are reduced by 5/9 of 1% for each month before full retirement age a fully insured worker retires, up to 36 months
- If a fully insured worker retires more than 36 months early, the benefit is reduced by 5/12 of 1% per month

---

INCREASED SOCIAL SECURITY BENEFITS FOR DELAYED RETIREMENT

- If born in 1933-1934, worker will receive annual benefit increase of 5.5% per year for delayed retirement
- If born in 1935-1936, worker will receive annual benefit increase of 6.0% per year for delayed retirement
- If born in 1937-1938, worker will receive annual benefit increase of 6.5% per year for delayed retirement
- If born in 1939-1940, worker will receive annual benefit increase of 7.0% per year for delayed retirement
- If born in 1941-1942, worker will receive annual benefit increase of 7.5% per year for delayed retirement
- If born in 1943 or later, worker will receive annual benefit increase of 8.0% per year for delayed retirement

SOCIAL SECURITY BENEFITS TAXATION

GROUPS EXEMPT FROM
SOCIAL SECURITY COVERAGE

SOCIAL SECURITY BENEFITS TAXATION

- If an insured worker receives other income in addition to social security benefits, a portion of the social security benefits will be taxable if MAGI exceeds certain limits
- For single taxpayers:
  - If MAGI is between $25,000 and $34,000 then 50% of social security benefits are taxable
  - If MAGI is greater than $34,000, then 85% of social security benefits are taxable
- For married taxpayers filing a joint return:
  - If MAGI is between $32,000 and $44,000, then 50% of social security benefits are taxable
  - If MAGI is greater than $44,000, then 85% of social security benefits are taxable

---

GROUPS EXEMPT FROM SOCIAL SECURITY COVERAGE

- College students enrolled in Federal Work-Study program
- Election workers earning less than $1,800 per year
- Federal employees hired before January 1, 1984
- Graduate students receiving stipends
- Household workers earning less than $2,100 per year
- Members of certain religious groups
- Minor children with earnings from household work
- Newspaper delivery persons under age 18
- Railroad employees
- State or local government employees hired before March 31, 1986 who participate in alternative retirement system

QUALIFIED RETIREMENT PLAN

QUALIFIED RETIREMENT PLAN LOANS

QUALIFIED RETIREMENT PLAN

- Retirement plan that meets the requirements of IRC section 401
- Employer is provided an immediate tax deduction for amounts contributed to the plan
- Employee does not pay current income tax on amounts contributed to the plan on his or her behalf
- Employer and employee contributions and investment earnings grow tax-free until distributed
- Employee withdrawals are generally not permitted before age 59 ½ without incurring a 10% penalty
- Two types of qualified retirement plans are defined contribution plans and defined benefit plans

---

QUALIFIED RETIREMENT PLAN LOANS

Loan from a qualified retirement plan must meet the following conditions:
- Must be adequately secured
- Must be available to all employees
- Must be offered according to plan documents
- Must be offered at a reasonable interest rate
- Term of the loan may not exceed five years unless the proceeds are used to acquire a primary residence for the employee

QUALIFIED RETIREMENT PLAN
DISTRIBUTION OPTIONS

DEFINED CONTRIBUTION PLAN

QUALIFIED RETIREMENT PLAN DISTRIBUTION OPTIONS

- Direct trustee-to-trustee transfer
- Lump sum distribution
- Payment in the form of an annuity or other periodic payment option
- Rollover of funds from one qualified retirement plan to another

---

DEFINED CONTRIBUTION PLAN

- Qualified retirement plan in which an employee's future benefits are variable
- Employee assumes the investment risk
- Employee assumes the risk of pre-retirement inflation
- Annual contributions to an employee's account are limited to the lesser of 25% of compensation or $56,000 in 2019
- Forfeitures may be used to reduce employer contributions or may be allocated to the accounts of remaining employees in a nondiscriminatory manner
- Two types of defined contribution plans are profit sharing plans and pension plans

DEFINED CONTRIBUTION PLAN VESTING

_____

21-AND-1 RULE

DEFINED CONTRIBUTION PLAN VESTING

- Employee contributions are 100% vested at all times
- Employer contributions to a defined contribution plan must use either the 3-year cliff vesting or 6-year graded vesting schedules
  - 3-year cliff vesting: An employee with at least 3 years of service is 100% vested. Vesting is not required before 3 years of service are completed.
  - 2 to 6-year graded vesting: Beginning at 2 years of service, an employee becomes 20% vested each year, so that he or she will become 100% vested after 6 years of service

----

21-AND-1 RULE

- Employees must be eligible to participate in an employer's qualified retirement plan within six months after the later of attaining age 21 or completing one year of service
- Employers can require two years of service if employees are 100% immediately vested upon eligibility
- One year of service is defined as any calendar year, plan year, or other consecutive 12-month period during which 1,000 hours of service are completed by an employee

PROFIT SHARING PLAN

401(k) PLAN

PROFIT SHARING PLAN

- Defined contribution plan that allows employees to share in company profits
- Annual contributions to a profit sharing plan are not mandatory but must be substantial and recurring
- Profit sharing plans are well-suited for companies with unstable cash flows
- Annual contributions to an employee's account are limited to the lesser of 25% of compensation or $56,000 in 2019
- Contributions are not required to be allocated on a pro-rata basis, but contributions cannot be discriminatory
- Profit sharing plans tend to favor younger employees
- Loans may be permitted

401(k) PLAN

- Type of profit sharing plan in which elective salary deferrals are made with pre-tax dollars and are excluded from an employee's taxable income
- Employee contributions are limited to $19,000 in 2019. An additional $6,000 may be contributed by employees over age 50.
- An employer may contribute to an employee's account and offer matching contributions, but total additions cannot exceed $56,000 per employee in 2019
- In-service withdrawals are subject to a 10% premature distribution penalty for employees under age 59 ½
- Distributions from a 401(k) plan following separation from service after attaining age 55 are not subject to the 10% premature distribution penalty

401(k) PLAN
HARDSHIP WITHDRAWALS

———————————

401(k) PLAN LOANS

401(k) PLAN
HARDSHIP WITHDRAWALS

- Hardship withdrawals from a 401(k) plan may be permitted, but an employee must first demonstrate to the plan administrator an immediate and heavy financial need
- Hardship withdrawals are limited to the amount of employee contributions, and do not include earnings or matching contributions
- Hardship withdrawals are subject to a 10% premature distribution penalty for employees under age 59 ½
- Following a hardship withdrawal, an employee is prohibited from making elective salary deferrals for a six-month period

----

401(k) PLAN LOANS

- The maximum loan permitted from a 401(k) plan is 50% of an employee's vested account balance, not to exceed $50,000
- A loan up to $10,000 may be permitted from a 401(k) plan even if it's greater than 50% of an employee's vested account balance
- Term of the loan may not exceed five years unless the proceeds are used to acquire a primary residence for the employee

403(b) PLAN

403(b) PLAN PARTICIPANTS

403(b) PLAN

- Also referred to as a tax-sheltered annuity (TSA) plan
- Elective salary deferrals are made with pre-tax dollars and are excluded from an employee's taxable income
- Employee contributions are limited to $19,000 in 2019. An additional $6,000 may be contributed by employees over age 50.
- An additional catch up contribution is permitted for employees with 15 years of service who have averaged less than $5,000 per year in elective salary deferrals
- An employer may contribute to an employee's account and offer matching contributions, but total additions cannot exceed $56,000 per employee in 2019
- In-service withdrawals are subject to a 10% premature distribution penalty for employees under age 59 ½

403(b) PLAN PARTICIPANTS

403(b) plan participants may include:
- Churches and religious organizations
- Not-for-profit hospitals
- Public schools
- State colleges
- Universities

457 PLAN

_____

457 PLAN PARTICIPANTS

457 PLAN

- Elective salary deferrals are made with pre-tax dollars and are excluded from an employee's taxable income
- Employee contributions are limited to $19,000 in 2019. An additional $6,000 may be contributed by employees over age 50.
- An additional catch up contribution is permitted for employees who are within three years of retirement if they have not contributed the maximum amount in prior years
- An employer may contribute to an employee's account and offer matching contributions, but total additions cannot exceed $56,000 per employee in 2019

---

457 PLAN PARTICIPANTS

457 plan participants may include:
- Nonprofit organizations
- State, county, and local government agencies
- Tax-exempt organizations

ESOP

ESOP USES

ESOP

- Employee stock ownership plan
- Defined contribution plan that invests primarily in company stock
- Employer establishes a trust for employees and either contributes cash to purchase shares of company stock, contributes shares directly, or has the plan borrow cash to purchase shares
- ESOPs may invest entirely in company stock
- Employer contributions to an ESOP are deductible in the year they are made to the plan
- Employees are taxed in the year the benefits are distributed or made available to them

---

ESOP USES

ESOPs are established to:
- Create a market for shares of a closely held corporation
- Meet the general financing requirements of a corporation
- Motivate, reward, and retain employees
- Transfer ownership of company stock to employees

STOCK BONUS PLAN

MONEY PURCHASE PLAN

STOCK BONUS PLAN

- Defined contribution plan designed to provide benefits similar to those of a profit sharing plan, except that benefits are distributed to employees in the form of stock rather than cash
- If an employee receives stock that is not traded on an established market, he or she may require the employer to repurchase the stock using a fair valuation formula
- Annual contributions are not mandatory but must be substantial and recurring
- Corporate ownership is diluted as shares of stock are granted to employees
- Employer contributions of stock are deductible up to 15% of covered payroll

---

MONEY PURCHASE PLAN

- Defined contribution pension plan that uses a fixed percentage of compensation formula to determine annual contributions to employee accounts
- Requires mandatory annual employer contributions
- In-service withdrawals are not permitted
- Loans are permitted
- Money purchase plans tend to favor younger employees

TARGET BENEFIT PLAN

DEFINED BENEFIT PLAN

TARGET BENEFIT PLAN

- Defined contribution pension plan that uses a fixed age-weighted formula to determine annual contributions to employee accounts
- Requires an actuarial calculation at the inception of the plan only
- Requires mandatory annual employer contributions
- In-service withdrawals are not permitted
- Loans are permitted
- Target benefit plans tend to favor older employees

DEFINED BENEFIT PLAN

- Qualified retirement plan in which an employee's future benefits are fixed and guaranteed
- Employer assumes the investment risk
- Employer assumes the risk of pre-retirement inflation
- Annual benefit is limited to $225,000 in 2019
- Forfeitures must be used to reduce employer contributions and may not be allocated to the accounts of remaining employees
- Defined benefit plans tend to favor older employees because the present value of the guaranteed benefit is greater as the time remaining until retirement decreases

DEFINED BENEFIT PLAN FUNDING

DEFINED BENEFIT PLAN VESTING

DEFINED BENEFIT PLAN FUNDING

- Higher than expected investment returns will reduce employer contributions
- Higher than expected employee turnover will reduce employer contributions
- Larger than expected forfeitures will reduce employer contributions
- Longer than expected life expectancy will increase employer contributions

---

DEFINED BENEFIT PLAN VESTING

- Employer contributions to a defined benefit plan must use either the 5-year cliff vesting or 7-year graded vesting schedules
  - 5-year cliff vesting: An employee with at least 5 years of service is 100% vested. Vesting is not required before 5 years of service are completed.
  - 3 to 7-year graded vesting: Beginning at 3 years of service, an employee becomes 20% vested each year, so that he or she will be 100% vested after 7 years of service

CASH BALANCE PLAN

PBGC

CASH BALANCE PLAN

- Defined benefit plan in which each employee's benefit is defined in terms of a stated account balance, similar to a defined contribution plan
- Each employee's account is credited annually with a pay credit and an interest credit
- Changes in the value of plan investments does not affect the benefit amounts promised to employees
- Cash balance plans tend to favor older employees

PBGC

- Pension Benefit Guaranty Corporation
- Government agency that guarantees minimum pension benefits to defined benefit plan participants whose plans have terminated due to insufficient funds

SUMMARY PLAN DESCRIPTION

———————————

SUMMARY PLAN
DESCRIPTION REQUIREMENTS

SUMMARY PLAN DESCRIPTION

- The Summary Plan Description (SPD) communicates the following information to qualified retirement plan participants:
    - When an employee may begin participating in the plan
    - How benefits are calculated
    - When benefits vest
    - How benefits are paid
    - How to file a claim for benefits

SUMMARY PLAN DESCRIPTION REQUIREMENTS

- The plan administrator is legally required to provide all participants with a copy of the Summary Plan Description (SPD)
- For new qualified retirement plans, the SPD must be provided to participants within 120 days after the plan has been established
- For existing qualified retirement plans, the SPD must be provided to new participants within 90 days after becoming eligible to enroll in the plan

FIDUCIARY

ROLES OF A FIDUCIARY

FIDUCIARY

- A fiduciary under the provisions of ERISA is any person that:
    - Exercises authority over plan administration
    - Exercises authority over plan management
    - Exercises authority over the disposition of plan assets
    - Provides investment advice for a fee or other compensation
- A fiduciary for a qualified retirement plan includes:
    - Plan administrator
    - Plan investment advisor
    - Plan sponsor
    - Plan trustee

ROLES OF A FIDUCIARY

- Roles of a fiduciary include:
    - Act solely in the interest of plan participants and their beneficiaries
    - Diversify plan investments
    - Pay only reasonable plan expenses
    - Prudently execute all duties
- If a fiduciary fails to meet the basic standards of conduct, he or she may be held personally liable for losses incurred by the plan

ERISA

PROHIBITED TRANSACTION

ERISA

- Employee Retirement Income Security Act
- Requires qualified retirement plan sponsors to disclose full and accurate information about plan activity to all participants
- ERISA establishes the following for qualified retirement plans:
  - Eligibility requirements
  - Fiduciary responsibilities
  - Minimum funding standards
  - Vesting requirements

PROHIBITED TRANSACTION

- A transaction between a plan and a disqualified person that is prohibited by law
- Prohibited transactions include:
  - Fiduciary using plan income or assets for his or her own benefit
  - Furnishing goods or services between a plan and a disqualified person
  - Lending money or extending credit between a plan and a disqualified person
  - Selling, exchanging, or leasing property between a plan and a disqualified person
  - Transferring plan income or assets to a disqualified person

LIFE INSURANCE IN A
QUALIFIED RETIREMENT PLAN

QUALIFIED RETIREMENT PLAN
DISCRIMINATION TESTING

LIFE INSURANCE IN A QUALIFIED RETIREMENT PLAN

- In a defined contribution plan, the premiums paid for whole life insurance may not exceed 50% of the contributions made to the plan on the participant's behalf
- In a defined contribution plan, the premiums paid for term, universal, or variable life insurance may not exceed 25% of the contributions made to the plan on the participant's behalf
- In a defined benefit plan, a participant's life insurance benefit may not exceed 100 times the participant's projected monthly retirement benefit

---

QUALIFIED RETIREMENT PLAN DISCRIMINATION TESTING

Qualified retirement plan discrimination tests include:
- Average benefits test
- Ratio percentage test
- 50/40 test

AVERAGE BENEFITS TEST

RATIO PERCENTAGE TEST

AVERAGE BENEFITS TEST

- For a qualified retirement plan to pass the average benefits test, the average benefit percentage of non-highly compensated employees must be at least 70% of the average benefit percentage of highly compensated employees

---

RATIO PERCENTAGE TEST

- For a qualified retirement plan to pass the ratio percentage test, the percentage of non-highly compensated employees who benefit under the plan must be at least 70% of the percentage of highly compensated employees who benefit under the plan

50/40 TEST

_____

HIGHLY COMPENSATED EMPLOYEE

50/40 TEST

- For a defined benefit plan to pass the 50/40 test, the plan must benefit at least the lesser of 50 employees or 40% of all employees

---

HIGHLY COMPENSATED EMPLOYEE

The following are considered highly compensated employees:
- 5% owner
- Employee with compensation exceeding $120,000 in 2018 will be considered highly compensated in 2019
- Employee with compensation exceeding $125,000 in 2019 will be considered highly compensated in 2020

KEY EMPLOYEE

TOP HEAVY PLAN

KEY EMPLOYEE

The following are considered key employees:
- 5% owner
- 1% owner with compensation exceeding $150,000 in 2019
- Officer with compensation exceeding $180,000 in 2019

———————————

TOP HEAVY PLAN

- A plan is top-heavy if more than 60% of total plan benefits are in favor of key employees
- If a defined contribution plan is top heavy, the minimum contribution the employer must make on behalf of non-key employees is 3% of each non-key employee's compensation
- If a defined benefit plan is top heavy, the minimum contribution the employer must make on behalf of non-key employees is equal to the lesser of 20%, or 2% per year of service, of each non-key employee's average compensation for the five highest consecutive years

PERMITTED DISPARITY IN A DEFINED CONTRIBUTION PLAN

PERMITTED DISPARITY IN A DEFINED BENEFIT PLAN

PERMITTED DISPARITY IN A DEFINED CONTRIBUTION PLAN

- Permitted disparity is used to skew retirement plan contributions in favor of highly compensated employees
- For a defined contribution plan, the maximum permitted disparity is the lesser of the base percentage or 5.7%
- Example:
  - ABC, Inc. adopts a defined contribution plan with a base percentage of 6.5%. Given the permitted disparity, what is the excess percentage?
  - The maximum permitted disparity in a defined contribution plan is the lesser of the base percentage (6.5%) or 5.7%
  - The excess percentage is 6.5% + 5.7% = 12.2%

PERMITTED DISPARITY IN A DEFINED BENEFIT PLAN

- Permitted disparity is used to skew retirement plan contributions in favor of highly compensated employees
- For a defined benefit plan, the maximum permitted disparity is the lesser of the base percentage or 26.25%
- Example:
  - ABC, Inc. adopts a defined benefit plan with a base percentage of 21.75%. Given the permitted disparity, what is the excess percentage?
  - The maximum permitted disparity in a defined benefit plan is the lesser of the base percentage (21.75%) or 26.25%
  - The excess percentage is 21.75% + 21.75% = 43.50%

TRADITIONAL IRA

TRADITIONAL IRA
DEDUCTION PHASEOUTS

TRADITIONAL IRA

- Contributions are limited to $6,000 in 2019. An additional $1,000 may be contributed by individuals over age 50.
- Contributions may be fully or partially deductible depending on the taxpayer's MAGI and tax-filing status
- Contributions and investment earnings grow tax-free until distributed
- Distributions are generally not permitted before age 59 ½ without incurring a 10% penalty
- Individuals over age 70 ½ cannot contribute to a traditional IRA
- A traditional IRA may be established and funded any time before April 15 of the calendar year following the year in which the contribution applies
- Loans are not permitted

TRADITIONAL IRA
DEDUCTION PHASEOUTS

MAGI phaseouts to deduct IRA contributions in 2019:
- $64,000 - $74,000 if single and an active participant in a qualified retirement plan
- $103,000 - $123,000 if married filing jointly and an active participant in a qualified retirement plan
- $193,000 - $203,000 if married filing jointly and the spouse of an active participant in a qualified retirement plan
- $0 - $10,000 if married filing separately and an active participant in a qualified retirement plan

TRADITIONAL IRA
ACTIVE PARTICIPANT STATUS

TRADITIONAL IRA
PROHIBITED INVESTMENTS

TRADITIONAL IRA
ACTIVE PARTICIPANT STATUS

- An active participant for purposes of deducting IRA contributions is any individual who actively participates in a qualified retirement plan, SEP, or SIMPLE
- For a defined contribution plan, an individual is considered an active participant if he or she makes elective or non-elective contributions to the plan
- For a defined benefit plan, an individual is considered an active participant if he or she participates in the plan or meets the eligibility requirements at any time during the plan year
- A participant in a 457 plan is not considered an active participant for purposes of deducting IRA contributions

---

TRADITIONAL IRA
PROHIBITED INVESTMENTS

- Antiques
- Art work
- Coins (except US-minted coins)
- Collectibles
- Gems
- Jewelry
- Metals
- Stamps

TRADITIONAL IRA
EXCESS CONTRIBUTIONS

IRA DISTRIBUTION FOR
FIRST-TIME HOME PURCHASE

TRADITIONAL IRA
EXCESS CONTRIBUTIONS

- The excise tax for over contributing to an IRA is 6%
- The excise tax is applied each year excess contributions remain in the account
- To avoid the excise tax, all excess contributions and investment earnings must be withdrawn before the due date of the federal income tax return

---

IRA DISTRIBUTION FOR
FIRST-TIME HOME PURCHASE

Penalty-free distributions from an IRA are permitted for a first-time home purchase if the following requirements are met:

- Home must be the taxpayer's primary residence
- Home must be purchased within 120 days of money being withdrawn from the IRA
- Money must be used only for qualified acquisition costs not exceeding a lifetime maximum of $10,000
- Taxpayer must not have owned a primary residence during the preceding two years

ROTH IRA

ROTH IRA
CONTRIBUTION PHASEOUTS

ROTH IRA

Roth IRAs are subject to the same rules that apply to traditional IRAs, except:
- Contributions are not deductible
- Contributions can be made beyond age 70 ½
- Contributions (not earnings) may be withdrawn at any age without incurring a 10% penalty
- Qualified distributions are tax-free
- Roth IRA owners are not required to take minimum distributions beginning at age 70 ½

ROTH IRA
CONTRIBUTION PHASEOUTS

MAGI phaseouts to contribute to a Roth IRA in 2017:
- $122,000 - $137,000 if single
- $193,000 - $203,000 if married filing jointly
- $0 - $10,000 if married filing separately

SIMPLE IRA

SIMPLE IRA ELIGIBILITY

SIMPLE IRA

- Savings Incentive Match Plan for Employees
- An IRA-based plan that allows employers to make contributions toward their employees' retirement, or toward their own retirement if self-employed
- Elective salary deferrals are made with pre-tax dollars and are excluded from an employee's taxable income
- Employee contributions are limited to $13,000 in 2019. An additional $3,000 may be contributed by employees over age 50.
- Employers make matching or nonelective contributions
- Employee contributions are 100% vested at all times
- Contributions and investment earnings grow tax-free until distributed

---

SIMPLE IRA ELIGIBILITY

- A SIMPLE IRA may only be established by employers who had no more than 100 employees who earned $5,000 or more in compensation during the preceding year
- A SIMPLE IRA may be established on any date between January 1 and October 1 of the plan year
- An employer cannot maintain any other qualified plan, 403(b) plan, or SEP at the same time it has a SIMPLE IRA in operation

SIMPLE IRA
EMPLOYER CONTRIBUTIONS

SIMPLE IRA
EARLY WITHDRAWALS

SIMPLE IRA
EMPLOYER CONTRIBUTIONS

Employer contributions to a SIMPLE IRA must meet the following requirements:

- The employer must match dollar for dollar the first 3% of compensation that eligible employees elect to defer, or
- The employer must make annual nonelective contributions of 2% of compensation for all eligible employees

---

SIMPLE IRA
EARLY WITHDRAWALS

- Early withdrawals from a SIMPLE IRA are subject to a 25% penalty if the withdrawals are made during the first two years of plan participation
- After the initial two-year period, the early withdrawal penalty is reduced to 10%
- The 25% penalty for early withdrawals does not apply to SIMPLE 401(k) plans. For SIMPLE 401(k) plans the early withdrawal penalty is a constant 10%.

SEP

SEP ELIGIBILITY

SEP

- Simplified Employee Pension
- An IRA-based plan that allows employers to make contributions toward their employees' retirement, or toward their own retirement if self-employed
- Annual contributions are limited to the lesser of 25% of compensation or $56,000 in 2019
- Contributions and investment earnings grow tax-free until distributed
- Contributions are 100% vested at all times
- Loans are not permitted
- Plans established prior to January 1, 1997 may allow salary deferral contributions. These plans are known as SARSEPs.

SEP ELIGIBILITY

- An employee must meet the following requirements to qualify for a SEP:
  - Must be at least 21 years old
  - Must have earned at least $600 in compensation during the year in 2019
  - Must have worked for the employer for at least three out of the five previous years
- A SEP may be established and funded any time before April 15 of the calendar year following the year in which the contribution applies

SUBSTANTIALLY EQUAL PERIODIC PAYMENTS (SEPP)

REQUIRED MINIMUM DISTRIBUTION

SUBSTANTIALLY EQUAL PERIODIC PAYMENTS (SEPP)

- If distributions from an IRA or qualified retirement plan are made as part of a series of substantially equal periodic payments over the participant's lifetime, the 10% premature distribution penalty does not apply
- Payments must continue for five years or until the participant reaches age 59 ½, whichever is longer
- There is no minimum age requirement to begin taking substantially equal periodic payments, and the IRS does not require a reason to begin taking payments

---

REQUIRED MINIMUM DISTRIBUTION

- The following plans are required to take RMDs: Employer sponsored retirement plans, traditional IRAs, SEPs, SARSEPs, and SIMPLE IRAs
  - RMDs are required from Roth 401(k) plans, but are not required from Roth IRAs while the account owner is alive
- RMDs begin the year the participant turns age 70 ½
  - The first RMD may be delayed until April 1 of the following year, but the participant must then take two distributions before December 31 of that year. All subsequent RMDs must be taken by December 31.
- There is a 50% excise tax on any amount that should have been distributed, but was not actually distributed

QUALIFIED PRERETIREMENT SURVIVOR ANNUITY (QPSA)

QUALIFIED JOINT AND SURVIVOR ANNUITY (QJSA)

QUALIFIED PRERETIREMENT SURVIVOR ANNUITY (QPSA)

- QPSA is a death benefit paid as a life annuity to the surviving spouse of a qualified retirement plan participant
- To qualify for a QPSA, the participant must have been vested in his or her retirement benefit at the time of death, and death must have occurred prior to retirement
- A spouse can waive his or her right to a QPSA by signing a waiver that is witnessed by a notary or plan representative

---

QUALIFIED JOINT AND SURVIVOR ANNUITY (QJSA)

- QJSA entitles the surviving spouse of a qualified retirement plan participant to receive periodic payments equal to at least 50% of the periodic payments the participant received during his or her lifetime
- A spouse can waive his or her right to a QJSA by signing a waiver that is witnessed by a notary or plan representative

QUALIFIED DOMESTIC RELATIONS ORDER (QDRO)

QDRO REQUIREMENTS

QUALIFIED DOMESTIC RELATIONS ORDER (QDRO)

- A court order for a retirement plan to pay child support or alimony to a spouse, former spouse, child, or other dependent of a retirement plan participant
- A spouse or former spouse that receives a QDRO benefit must report the benefit as if he or she was the plan participant
- A QDRO distribution that is paid directly to a child or other dependent is taxed to the plan participant

---

QDRO REQUIREMENTS

A QDRO must contain the following information:
- Name and address of the participant
- Name and address of each payee
- Name of each plan to which the order applies
- Dollar amount or percentage of the participant's benefit that is to be paid to each payee
- Period of time to which the order applies

EMPLOYEE BENEFITS

TAXABLE FRINGE BENEFITS

NONTAXABLE FRINGE BENEFITS

TAXABLE FRINGE BENEFITS

- Any fringe benefit provided to an employee is taxable and must be included in the employee's pay unless it is specifically excluded under Section 2 of IRS Publication 15-B.

NONTAXABLE FRINGE BENEFITS

Section 2 of IRS Publication 15-B excludes all or part of the value of the following fringe benefits from an employee's pay:

- Accident and health benefits
- Achievement awards
- Adoption assistance
- Athletic facilities
- De minimis benefits
- Dependent care assistance
- Educational assistance
- Employee discounts
- Employee stock options
- Employer-provided phones
- Group-term life insurance
- Health savings accounts
- Lodging on business premises
- Meals
- No-additional-cost services
- Retirement planning services
- Transportation benefits
- Tuition reduction
- Working condition benefits

GROUP TERM LIFE INSURANCE

GROUP TERM LIFE INSURANCE TAXATION

GROUP TERM LIFE INSURANCE

- Employee life insurance that remains in effect until employment is terminated or until a specific term expires
- The amount of coverage provided to each employee must be based on a formula that prevents individual selection. The formula may be based on the employee's age, compensation, position, or years of service.
- Evidence of insurability is not required to qualify for coverage
- Coverage is provided through a master contract between the employer and the insurance company. Each employee receives a certificate as evidence of coverage.

GROUP TERM LIFE INSURANCE TAXATION

- There are no tax consequences to the employee if the total amount of coverage does not exceed $50,000
- The cost for coverage exceeding $50,000 must be included in the employee's income based on the figures from the IRS premium table
- An employer can deduct contributions to a group term life insurance plan regardless of the amount of coverage it provides

GROUP TERM LIFE INSURANCE CONVERSION

_____

GROUP PAID-UP LIFE INSURANCE

GROUP TERM LIFE INSURANCE CONVERSION

- A terminated employee may convert his or her group term policy to an individual whole life policy without providing evidence of insurability
- Former employees have 31 days following termination of employment to apply for conversion
- The amount of whole life coverage after conversion may not exceed the amount of coverage that was provided through the group term policy
- The premium for whole life coverage is based on the employee's age on the conversion date

---

GROUP PAID-UP LIFE INSURANCE

- Employee life insurance coverage that consists of increasing units of permanent insurance and decreasing units of term insurance
- The death benefit remains level each year. As the amount of paid-up insurance (purchased by the employee) increases over time, the amount of term insurance (purchased by the employer) decreases.

DEPENDENT GROUP LIFE INSURANCE

GROUP DISABILITY INSURANCE

DEPENDENT GROUP
LIFE INSURANCE

- Life insurance coverage provided on the lives of an employee's dependents
- Eligible insureds include the employee's spouse and unmarried dependent children. If coverage is elected, all dependents meeting the definition must be insured to prevent adverse selection.
- There are no tax consequences to the employee if the total amount of coverage does not exceed $2,000 per insured
- The cost for coverage exceeding $2,000 per insured must be included in the employee's income based on the figures from the IRS premium table

---

GROUP DISABILITY INSURANCE

- Employee disability insurance that remains in effect until employment is terminated
- Provides a disabled employee with an annual benefit up to 70% of his or her pre-disability income
- Evidence of insurability is not required to qualify for coverage
- Premiums are deductible by the employer and benefits are taxable to the employee

GROUP HEALTH INSURANCE

COBRA

GROUP HEALTH INSURANCE

- Premiums are deductible by the employer and benefits are tax-free to the employee
- Premiums paid by an employer are excluded from an employee's income if any of the following individuals are covered:
  - The employee, if currently employed
  - The employee, if retired
  - The employee's spouse
  - The employee's dependent child

COBRA

- Consolidated Omnibus Budget Reconciliation Act
- Allows employees who have lost their job to continue receiving identical health coverage that was provided through their group health insurance plan
- Evidence of insurability is not required to qualify for COBRA
- Employers with 20 or more employees must offer COBRA
- Qualified individuals must pay the employer's share of insurance premiums, but the total cost may not exceed 102% of the total cost for providing the same coverage to similarly situated employees
- Employers must pay a non-deductible excise tax of $100 per day for failing to notify a qualified individual about the right to elect COBRA coverage

COBRA ELIGIBILITY

COBRA BENEFIT PERIOD

COBRA ELIGIBILITY

- Qualified individuals have 60 days following a qualifying event to elect COBRA coverage
- The following individuals are eligible for COBRA:
  - Employees who are voluntarily or involuntarily terminated for reasons other than gross misconduct
  - Employees who have changed from full-time to part-time status
  - Spouses and other dependents of a covered employee who have lost health coverage due to the employee's death, divorce, legal separation, or eligibility for Medicare
  - Children of a covered employee who have lost health coverage due to the loss of dependent status caused by age limitations or marriage

---

COBRA BENEFIT PERIOD

- The maximum COBRA benefit period is 18 months if the qualifying event is termination of employment or reduced work hours
- If a qualified individual is considered disabled (as determined by social security) within the first 60 days after receiving COBRA coverage, he or she may extend the COBRA benefit period to a total of 29 months
- The maximum COBRA benefit period is 36 months if the qualifying event is death or divorce from a covered employee

GROUPS EXEMPT FROM COBRA

_____

FLEXIBLE SPENDING ACCOUNT (FSA)

GROUPS EXEMPT FROM COBRA

The following employers are not required to offer COBRA:
- Employers with less than 20 employees
- Church employers
- Government employers

FLEXIBLE SPENDING ACCOUNT (FSA)

- Account established through an employer that reimburses employees for qualified medical expenses incurred during the period of coverage
- At the beginning of the plan year, the employee must determine how much he or she will contribute to an FSA. The account is funded through employee salary deferrals.
- Employee contributions are not subject to payroll tax
- Contributions made by an employer on behalf of an employee are excluded from gross income
- Distributions from an FSA are tax-free if used to pay for qualified medical expenses
- "Use it or lose it." Amounts remaining in an FSA at the end of the plan year will be forfeited.

HEALTH SAVINGS ACCOUNT (HSA)

HEALTH SAVINGS ACCOUNT ELIGIBILITY

HEALTH SAVINGS ACCOUNT (HSA)

- Tax-exempt trust or custodial account established with a qualified HSA trustee to pay or reimburse a participant for qualified medical expenses
- The maximum contribution for single coverage is $3,500 in 2019. The maximum contribution for family coverage is $7,000 in 2019.
- Contributions are deductible
- Contributions and investment earnings grow tax-free
- Distributions from an HSA are tax-free if used to pay for qualified medical expenses
- Amounts remaining in an HSA at the end of the year will be carried over to the following year

---

HEALTH SAVINGS
ACCOUNT ELIGIBILITY

Participants must meet the following requirements to qualify for an HSA:

- Must be covered under a compatible high deductible health plan
- Must not be enrolled in Medicare
- Cannot be claimed as a dependent by another taxpayer
- Cannot have any other health coverage in place

VEBA

NONQUALIFIED DEFERRED COMPENSATION

VEBA

- Voluntary Employee Beneficiary Association
- Irrevocable tax-exempt trust that funds a variety of employee benefits including health insurance, life insurance, severance pay, and child care costs
- A VEBA may be established directly by an employer or through a collective bargaining agreement

---

NONQUALIFIED DEFERRED COMPENSATION

- Provides employees with customized retirement plan benefits
- Avoids qualified retirement plan nondiscrimination rules
- May provide benefits in excess of qualified retirement plan limits
- The employer is permitted a tax deduction when the benefit is included in the employee's income
- Employee is not required to pay tax on deferred amounts until the benefit is actually or constructively received
- For an employee to defer taxes on an NQDC plan, the plan must be unfunded, informally funded, or subject to substantial risk of forfeiture

SUBSTANTIAL RISK
OF FORFEITURE

CONSTRUCTIVE RECEIPT DOCTRINE

SUBSTANTIAL RISK
OF FORFEITURE

- Substantial risk of forfeiture exists if an employee's right to receive compensation is contingent upon the future performance of substantial services
- For example, if an employee's right to receive compensation is contingent upon his or her continued employment for a specific period of time, then substantial risk of forfeiture exists
- If substantial risk of forfeiture exists, an employee is not required to pay tax on deferred amounts until the benefit is actually or constructively received
- Death and disability are not adequate reasons to create substantial risk of forfeiture

---

CONSTRUCTIVE RECEIPT DOCTRINE

- Doctrine that states an employee will be immediately taxed on any compensation that he or she has the right to receive upon request without any risk of forfeiture
- To avoid constructive receipt, the employee's risk of forfeiture must be real and substantial
- In an NQDC plan, if an employee has the right to receive compensation but declines, the IRS will treat the compensation as constructively received

FUNDED PLAN

_____

UNFUNDED PLAN

FUNDED PLAN

- An NQDC plan is considered "funded" if assets are set aside from the claims of the company's creditors, and participants can expect future benefits to be paid from the segregated account
- For example, an NQDC plan is funded if assets are set aside in a trust or escrow account to pay future benefits
- If an NQDC plan is funded, participants are immediately taxed on the benefit amount, even though the benefit may not be immediately received

---

UNFUNDED PLAN

- An NQDC plan is considered "unfunded" if participants have only the employer's promise to pay benefits sometime in the future
- For an NQDC plan to be unfunded, participants must not have any rights or secured interest in the benefit. This ensures the participants avoid constructive receipt.

INFORMALLY FUNDED PLAN

SALARY CONTINUATION PLAN

INFORMALLY FUNDED PLAN

- An NQDC plan is considered "informally funded" if assets are set aside in a general reserve fund to meet the benefit obligations of the plan
- For example, an NQDC plan is informally funded if an employer transfers funds into a trust that remains part of the company's general assets and subject to the claims of the company's creditors
- For an NQDC plan to be informally unfunded, participants must not have any rights or secured interest in the benefit. This ensures the participants avoid constructive receipt.

SALARY CONTINUATION PLAN

- A plan in which the employee does not give up current compensation in exchange for receiving a benefit. Instead, the employee's salary continues and additional compensation is provided by the employer.
- When the benefit is paid, the employer receives a tax deduction and the benefit is recognized as ordinary income by the employee

SALARY REDUCTION PLAN

EXCESS BENEFIT PLAN

SALARY REDUCTION PLAN

- Also referred to as a pure deferred compensation plan
- A plan in which the employee gives up a portion of current compensation in exchange for receiving a future benefit equal to the amount deferred plus a predetermined rate of return
- When the benefit is paid, the employer receives a tax deduction and the benefit is recognized as ordinary income by the employee

---

EXCESS BENEFIT PLAN

- A plan that provides benefits to an employee in excess of the limitations on contributions and benefits imposed by IRC section 415
- To avoid current taxation to the employee, the plan must be unfunded or informally funded

RABBI TRUST

SECULAR TRUST

RABBI TRUST

- Irrevocable trust established by an employer to provide nonqualified deferred compensation benefits to employees
- Employer contributions to the trust are subject to the claims of the company's creditors
- Employees are not in constructive receipt of the employer's contribution and are therefore not immediately taxed. When benefits are paid from the trust, the amount is recognized as ordinary income by employees and is deductible by the employer.
- Provides protection for employees in the event of a hostile takeover or merger
- A rabbi trust may not include a bankruptcy trigger

SECULAR TRUST

- Irrevocable trust established by an employer to provide nonqualified deferred compensation benefits to employees
- Employer contributions to the trust are not subject to the claims of the company's creditors
- Employees are in constructive receipt of the employer's contribution and are immediately taxed. The employer receives an immediate tax deduction for the amount contributed to the trust.
- Provides protection for employees in the event of an employer's bankruptcy, insolvency, merger, or takeover

DEATH BENEFIT ONLY (DBO) PLAN

RESTRICTED STOCK PLAN

DEATH BENEFIT ONLY (DBO) PLAN

- A plan in which all benefits are payable upon the death of an employee to his or her designated beneficiary
- The amount of life insurance used to fund a DBO plan is generally determined by a multiple of salary formula
- Premiums paid for life insurance used to fund a DBO plan are not deductible by the employer, but the death benefit received by the employer is tax-free. The employer then uses the death benefit to make payments to the employee's beneficiary. The payments are deductible by the employer and recognized as ordinary income by the beneficiary.

———————————

RESTRICTED STOCK PLAN

- A plan that provides employees with shares of company stock that are subject to certain restrictions or limitations before they may be sold
- Restrictions may include:
  - Employee may not engage in competition with a competitor
  - Employee must meet specific sales goals
  - Employee must remain employed for a specific period of time
- Restrictions are intended to retain employees and discourage misconduct
- When no longer subject to substantial risk of forfeiture, the employer receives a tax deduction and the benefit is recognized as ordinary income by the employee

PHANTOM STOCK PLAN

———————————

STOCK APPRECIATION RIGHT (SAR)

PHANTOM STOCK PLAN

- A plan that provides employees with the benefits of stock ownership without providing actual shares of company stock
- Benefit amounts are measured by the increase in value of company stock
- Phantom stock plans do not dilute existing shareholders because actual shares of stock are not exchanged
- No income is recognized on the date phantom stock is awarded
- When benefits are paid, the employer receives a tax deduction and the benefit is recognized as ordinary income by the employee

---

STOCK APPRECIATION RIGHT (SAR)

- A right that provides employees with a benefit equal to the increase in value of company stock between the date of grant and the exercise date
- Benefits may be paid in cash or stock
- When a SAR is exercised, the employer receives a tax deduction and the benefit is recognized as ordinary income by the employee
- SARS are commonly offered in tandem with stock options

EMPLOYEE STOCK
PURCHASE PLAN (ESPP)

INCENTIVE STOCK OPTION (ISO)

EMPLOYEE STOCK PURCHASE PLAN (ESPP)

- A plan that provides employees with the right to purchase shares of company stock during a specific period at a predetermined price
- The maximum discount permitted is 15% of the stock's fair market value
- The maximum value of stock an employee may purchase in any calendar year is $25,000
- The employee is not taxed at the time of grant or when an ESPP option is exercised. At the time of sale, the benefit may be taxed as capital gains if certain rules similar to those of ISOs are met.

INCENTIVE STOCK OPTION (ISO)

- A right to purchase shares of company stock that meets the requirements of IRC section 422
- ISOs may only be granted to employees and are not transferable except upon death
- The exercise price of an ISO must be at least equal to the fair market value of the stock when the option is granted
- Only the first $100,000 of ISO stock granted to a single employee each year is entitled to ISO tax treatment
- An employee holding an ISO must remain employed from date of grant until three months before date of exercise
- Stock must be held at least one year from the date of exercise and two years from the date of grant
- An ISO cannot be exercised more than ten years after the date of grant

INCENTIVE STOCK OPTION (ISO) TAXATION

NONQUALIFIED STOCK OPTION (NQSO)

INCENTIVE STOCK OPTION (ISO) TAXATION

- Example: Assume an ISO is granted to an employee providing the right to purchase 1,000 shares of company stock for $10 per share
- What are the tax consequences if the employee exercises the option when the stock's fair market value is $20 per share?
  - No tax is paid (AMT preference item)
- What are the tax consequences if the employee sells the stock for $30 per share after holding for two years?
  - ($30 - $10) x 1,000 shares = $20,000
  - $20,000 x capital gains rate = tax paid

NONQUALIFIED STOCK OPTION (NQSO)

- Unlike ISOs, NQSOs do not have to meet specific holding period requirements
- The exercise price of an NQSO may be less than the fair market value of the stock when the option is granted
- NQSOs may be granted to employees, family members, members of a board, independent contractors, and consultants
- NQSOs may be transferred or gifted to family members, trusts, and charities

NONQUALIFIED STOCK OPTION (NQSO) TAXATION

NONQUALIFIED STOCK OPTION (NQSO) TAXATION

- Example: Assume an NQSO is granted to an employee providing the right to purchase 1,000 shares of company stock for $10 per share
- What are the tax consequences if the employee exercises the option when the stock's fair market value is $20 per share?
    - ($20 - $10) x 1,000 shares = $10,000
    - $10,000 x ordinary income tax rate = tax paid
- What are the tax consequences if the employee sells the stock for $30 per share after holding for two years?
    - ($30 - $20) x 1,000 shares = $10,000
    - $10,000 x capital gains rate = tax paid

———————————

ABOUT THE AUTHOR

Matthew Brandeburg is a Certified Financial Planner in Columbus, Ohio. He serves as the Chief Operating Officer for a fee-only financial planning firm with over $700 million in assets under management and he's an active member of the National Association of Personal Financial Advisors (NAPFA). Matthew is the author of the books "Financial Planning For Your First Job," "Your Guide to the CFP Certification Exam," and "CFP Certification Exam Practice Question Workbook." In addition, he teaches the class "Financial Planning in your 20s and 30s" at Ohio State University.

INDEX